Tide Roaring In

For Terry +
George

Oh how great
to have you as
neighbors!

Adele Bourne

Tide Roaring In

Poems by

Adele MacVeagh Bourne

Kelsay Books

Cover: *theterramarproject@ flikr*

ISBN 13: 978-1-945752-17-9

Kelsay Books
Aldrich Press
www.kelsaybooks.com

In loving memory of Diana Kate Clurman, 1964-1987,
and of her father, Rodney Hart Clurman, 1933-1995

Acknowledgments

I would like to thank the journals listed below for publication of the following poems, some in previous versions.

Bryn Mawr Alumnae Bulletin: "Refugee Guest of the College"
Frequency Writers Missing Providence Anthology: "Morning Glory" and "Silent Meeting"
Mad Poets Review: "New Hampshire Woods" and "Falls Church Victory Garden"
New Brunswick Library Anthology: "Jefferson Hospital Cafeteria"
The Pedestal Magazine: "May Day"
Poetry Ink: "Life Guard"
South Mountain Anthology: "Eight Years Old"
Up and Under: "Mindfulness"
U.S. 1 Worksheets: "Black Wings," "From Afar," "Interview at the Annual Meeting of the Corporation," "The River," "The Salt Marsh," "Throwing Out Cookbooks," and "Advice to Writers: Sure-Fire Topics for Best Sellers."

Meg Clurman, Mark, Skyler, Alex, and Lena Patrick; Andrew, Claire, Kate, Emmeline, and Nate Clurman; Allen Freeman, Courtney Delph, and Reagan Freeman: where would I be without you?

And most especially, I would thank my very good friend, Nancy Scott, poet, artist, and longtime editor of U.S, 1 Worksheets, who encouraged me to put together this book in the first place, and then helped me organize and edit it. Her confidence in me, her experience, judgment, and assistance, have been invaluable. And I am extremely grateful for her interest and generous effort.

Contents

PART III

The Eagle

Come bird of the heaven and rest in my branches,
eat of my berries and wild honey hollows.
Soothe your warm feathers against my smooth bark
and wash away dust in the dew of my leaves.

For the way from one pole to another is wearying.
Currents you ride can twist into tempest
and the sun which gives life can fiercely withdraw it.

I am a tree dwarfed in your far sight,
roots deep in the soil as your wings sweep the skies.
Yet here I wait because I know you will need me
when down from the high silence you glide.

Before the great darkness blots out your bearings,
by the stars' faint light seek your eyrie.
Tuck head under wing because even for eagles
there is time for sleep and time to begin.

PART I

Insomnia

Four a.m.—Snow begins.
Squirrels dream of nuts
buried in our window boxes.

Five a.m.—Beyond dark firs
sky reflects bright clouds of snow
sparkling below Christmas lights.

Six a.m.—Japanese maple
raps her knuckles against the pane.
Glazed branches glow apricot.

Beneath the Snow

Move moles and voles,
rabbits and chipmunks
through huge, six-sided crystals
on their way to each other's bunks,
but the mice
tunnel up through the ice
peer about like little pistols,
until, chilled to rosiness,
they slide back home; their holes
for air and for adventure
to taunt the hawks,
and mock the hungry crows
who have no access
to subnivean coziness.

The River

When two people have loved each other,
what remains is the river between them,
direction, boundary, and source.

Come flood and disaster,
withdrawal, and mud,
the river waits out ice and scorch.

When the water roars over stones,
pushing a winter of driftwood,
eroding the banks where they stand,

the reasonable fear of drowning
forces them into retreat
to harder and drier ground.

Then, quiet and early sun
draws them back to the brink,
as the river gracefully settles

to a smooth and slower flow,
yielding a twinned reflection,
surrounded by woods and sky.

New Hampshire Woods

Great wolf pines arch over
the old logging road edged with wintergreen,
bearberry, encyclopedia of mushrooms.

There, fresh bear scat and a glimpse,
in underbrush, of mother and cub
loping from summer hollow to winter cave.

We freeze, walk slowly backward,
listen for crack of stick
under thunderous hum of mosquitoes.

Behind us white birches
glimmer green as last rays of the sun
burn the water.

As we reach the clearing,
Mars and Venus punch through cobalt sky.
Supper on the porch in the moonlight.

Down by the waterhole
coyotes yowl.
This year they've killed all the cats.

Quiet for hours. *A-broooo-hoooo!*
A moose bellows for a mate
Again and again. No reply.

All this hunger, all this breathing
shape us as we dream. Silently,
we find each other in the dark.

Nine-Thirty P.M.

for John

You said you'd be home by seven
after meeting an old friend for a drink
in the city twenty miles away.
Knowing my terrors you usually call,
but the temperature is ten degrees
and you are driving your old convertible,
that doesn't shift out of second, only once caught fire.
I assume the police will notify me.
You've been freelancing. No insurance.
Burying you will be possible, but expensive.
But who would play, "The Whoopee Hat Brigade,"
or tease me about the spiders in the corners,
or pour me a glass of wine and go change my flat tire
on a night as cold as this one, or pick up the check,
"Who has the shark bladder?" or interject
when the conversation turns to famine and war,
"Have you seen *Big Nose*, the first Eskimo pornographic film?"
As always when I admit you are irreplaceable,
your car chugs into the driveway, and there you are,
as irrepressibly alive as ever.

Problem Solver

Did put your French blueberry jam behind
the mayonnaise—

Too hard to find!

Did toss two hundred issues of the New
Yorker that you—

…still planned to read!

Did not stop complaining of the nine old
boats you dry-docked in the yard,
or when you bought yet one more

classic car…a bit of restoration!

Yet Coast Guard trained,
you'd drive on through the flames,
at home, abroad, wherever you were needed,
deflecting conflagration, directing mediation,
celebrating compromise when you succeeded.

Then you'd come home which became a home
for the rest of us when you arrived.

Refugee Guest of the College

He sat in the drawing room after lunch,
after coffee and liqueurs
with a blue flower in his hand.

We had work to do and exams to grade
and still he went on talking, the old Hungarian
once Hussar under the Austrian crown.
How pleasant and how civilized and how such good
beef borscht was so very hard to find; about American
theater and about Petöfi, the poet of his heartland
to whom freedom was red wine.

We'd never read Petöfi, so instead he quoted
Shakespeare with sibilants we strained to understand.
Trains to catch, and still this quiet guest kept talking
in capital letter English—French and German interspersed.

I have put on fifty pounds ten weeks inside this country.
His borrowed tweeds still hung loose on his six-foot frame.

My two children have been killed.
My grandchildren are imprisoned.
I taught at the University until the day
they smashed my teeth.

There was no more conversation.
Staring out the window, he said at last,
But it is late. I go.

We thanked him for his company,
returned to Robert Walpole and his
connivance with the king.

Vision in the Dark Age

for LT

Why did he turn the continent of himself,
that jungle of white cockatoos and lizards,
of mandrills, proud possessors of rainbow behinds,
with a slight twist of axis at my approach,
into the entire Antarctic?

Because he knew I cannot devour,
much less digest, penguin? They don't fly.
Listen, I won't scoop him up, blast him off the globe,
leave for outer space. Soon I would have sizzled down
to a mere meteorological souvenir.

*

In a vision he appeared last night,
eyes wild, button-down collar open at the throat
revealing a triple strand of pearls
gleaming against a camisole of blush pink silk.
What a weekend, he exclaimed.

I turned back the covers of my bed.
He laid down beside me, fully clothed.
I was wearing a modest, blue-striped, flannel affair
with YALE stitched on the pocket.

After a time, he got up and left for the far right wing
of our eminent school, but I could see
his light burning as he bent and wrote.
Then I awoke, looked at the clock—three a.m.

Next day, in the flesh, hair blazing like a comet,
he tells me over coffee in the faculty room
that he had driven home miserable at three a.m.,
and he looked at me with mirrors in his eyes.
Such penguins!

I cannot smash this glass
or sympathize or make him laugh…
Or tell him of my dream.
Alas, he is not my kind of explorer.

Commencement Farewell

You do have talent, my dear Miss Abbott.
You must not hesitate to put yourself forward,
even from the back of the room. Push hard.
I've seen you win at dominoes.
Go forth with your head held high.
You will travel a long way. Begin now.
Yes, once we could have been life-long friends
but that time is over. As for your fiancé,
leave him to me. Well, actually,
I must now, at last, admit, you already have.

Falls Church Victory Garden

After a 60-hour week at the War Department,
      Pa ploughed the red Virginia dirt, planted peas,
corn, beets, potatoes, and, to our disgust, rutabagas.
      You'll be glad to have them when the Germans
surrender and the Russians invade, he told us.
      We figured if anyone knew, he did, so we weeded,
picked off bugs, helped our mother—
      best damn farm wife ever born on Park Avenue—
who canned tomatoes, made bread, stretched ration books.

This decrepit place, only rental available, had a barn.
      To aid the war effort, my older sister raised
bantam hens whose eggs were the size of thimbles
      and begged Pa for a horse.
Stopping a trailer on the way to the slaughterhouse,
      Pa rescued Yankee for 75 dollars.
God damn horse has to earn his keep, he said.
      To cart manure to the fields,
he built a wagon from parts of an old buggy
      and boards he found behind the garage.

After he cut parts according to plan, he laid the bed
      on the framework, but forgot to nail it down.
Hand near the bit, he forced Yankee between the shafts,
      clambered up like a charioteer, slapped the reins.
Don John of Austria is riding to the wars!
      The horse bolted. Pa kept his balance,
but the wagon fell apart, piece by piece,
      just like my mother did, that spring of '44.

Veterans in Vermont

The semi turned left into the driveway.
Its trailer, barring the narrow mountain road,
carried as cargo a Boston Whaler,
a float filled with old sailors,
proudly in uniform for the Memorial Day Parade.

Suddenly, a red Maserati
roared up over the hill,
dove under the flatbed of the truck,
slid between titanic tires,
braked before the driver could be decapitated.

It reversed before torpedoing the sailors
onto dry land, then shot off as recklessly
as it had arrived, leaving the men
dazed but alive to realize that in peace,
as in war, they had been spared.

Naming Names

9/11/2001

My nephew Nick called on that calm, blue
New Hampshire morning.
Tell Mom I got out okay. Others need the phone.
I turned on the radio, woke my sister,
tried to reach our son.
Late that night, at last, we learned Andrew was safe.

9/11/2002

At the Town Hall,
we gathered to sing the *Messiah*,
then stood to read the names
of those who could be named—
a few were familiar.

9/11/2015

Silent Quaker Meeting.
White-haired men, women, young child
on the facing bench.
Heads bowed. Girls in bright dresses.
Upper gallery filled with modest ghosts.
Through the tall windows, century-old trees,
goldfinches, robins at the feeders.

Banners flap—*Drone Free Zone*
Black pinwheels spin.
One for each child who died last summer.
Muhammed Aba' Khan, aged 2 ½.

May Day

The country is at war.
She can't clean or cook or think.
Squirrels chase each other down a holly tree,
winding like silver ribbons through the green.

At an outdoor café,
she lunches with May, a former pupil
now fresh from the hospital
where her roommate hanged herself.

May hadn't liked the hospital.
She's seen Satan in the bathroom.
Telling this, her eyes glow red.
But—good news—she's been saved!

Pulling from her bag a Bible
bristling with bookmarks,
May reads aloud to her old teacher
and confides,

"You are my best friend."
Flowering cherries sway
like prom dresses.
Violets bend in the breeze.

Her daughter had been May's age
and suffered the same disease.
She wants to spit on a handkerchief,
as her own mother used to, wipe the milk

from the corners of May's mouth,
send her demons chattering off
to the squirrels overhead.
But she's no savior.

She hugs May, waves goodbye,
goes home exhausted. TV reports
the bombing of a school bus
full of girls wearing head scarves.

She decides on a nap, and dreams
of a luncheon at the White House,
which she attends, dressed
as a beautiful white horse.

PART II

If Poetry Could Do What Science Does

The SARS virus was found in six masked palm civets
. . . and in the only raccoon dog tested . . .
New York Times, June 15, 2007

I'd teach a young girl Mandarin.
She'd answer my questions
in a Dravidian dialect
we both understood.

In the morning, she'd read me
her latest verse, a psalm
whose key imagery would set free
the masked palm civets
and raccoon dogs languishing
cage upon cage in Chinese markets.

They'd beat their retreat
back to their lairs in the Himalayas,
calming our fears, curtailing
a pandemic that might cause
the deaths of forty million
there, and here.

In gratitude,
all those armed
would put down their weapons,
forswear harm,
share their food,
and take up poetry.

Pleased with our work, we'd say
goodbye. I'd collect my pile
of dictionaries, head for dinner,

but would find myself
no longer hungry, somehow fed
with an odd sense of completion.

My Revision

I was trying to rewrite my epic poem,
but one section I'd scribbled all over.
No matter what I did I couldn't make it right.
Instead, I thought I would bake a cake,
two-layer chocolate with a light cream filling
and raspberry icing decorated with rosettes.
And then I thought I could pin another page
on a tree so that the people strolling by
or sitting under it would look up and see my poem.
Perhaps an accompaniment for every canto:
watermelon, ice cold.

Damon the Seeker

Desperately in love with the quintuplets,
despairing because he could not project
himself into holograms,
Damon sought an interview,

not with Studio Boss
of Super Pixilated, Incorporated,
but with God Himself, not Roarer of Thunderstorms,

or Yahweh of Tidal Wave,
but with Bubba God from around the corner,
wearing a Tie with Blue and Green Bubbles
that matched his Bubble Socks.

"Not that I don't love matchy-matchy,
but how do you manage it, God?
So many of them, only one of you;
yet for me no others will do!"

 "Set them like a diamond
with five facets to catch the sun
on a platinum merry-go-round
with you as calliope.
Then carousel.
There may be spin off,
cream soda and pastrami,
but don't ask them why."

"That makes no sense at all."

"Just so. Bless you, my boy."

Date with a Muse

Have you ever been to Mardi Gras?
And if not, will you come with me?
What kind of costume will you choose?—
the hippopotamus, deadliest creature of the Nile,
or will you go instead, perhaps
as my Hypotenuse?

Yo, Poet Guy!

You sure do shred my pipe,
ream me with a T bar,
shoot out my lights
with your Japanese pellet gun PhD.
What a fakie tailside flip 180 out
critique in boiler plate
just so you get your comments done
before the weekend.

About my verse, you advised:
Not rewriting, but writing,
not writing, but re-imagining,
to pursue the TRUTH, the only aim of art,
and worth one's life.

I compared my note
with the ones you wrote
to the nubile junior members
of our seminar—each one
an Emily Dickinson
or a lively Sylvia Plath.

Guru of Germantown,
Shakespeare down the shore,
Bard of the bars of Manayunk,
faded jeans draped just so
over a drinker's shrinking loins.
They make it clear
nobody's cooking for you now.

Yeah, *you*, Jimmy Dean,
thirty years too late.

Fourth Letter by Emily to Her Master

Oh, did I offend It—whatever *draws* Us close when far apart—
that Thread wound round—unearned but given?
Did Daisy offend It—by not giving her Life—
as well as Spirit Knowledge?
This Spirit Love, Sir, is all that Daisy has.

What can she do to make her Master glad?

Something to do for Love—of Spider Silk—of Cobweb Fire—
to spring to Life—to Memory—what War so muddies over?
Bring Buttercup—Robin's Nest—
after Battle—after Sickroom— after Death
back to Mind.

For Someone Else to find.

Interview after the Annual Meeting
of the Corporation

for NA

When did you become aware
the world may not continue past
your last breath?
And what did you decide to do about it—
hasten or prevent?
Do you think that your apprehension of apocalypse
may be connected to what's playing at the multiplex?
Or to selling those mineral rights
in North Dakota by the base
with the subterranean nuclear missiles ?
You know, of course,
fracking can cause earthquakes?
Is this how you plan to pay the tuition
for all your children's MBAs
so they can rule the world in the future,
should one remain?

Morning Glory

Children came around because she listened to herself.
Indifferent to appearances, she did as she pleased,

wrote songs in Portuguese she'd picked up on the playground,
performed on the gamelan, clavier, drums.

Teens talked to her of problems with their great pulsations.
Young men loved her and she loved each in turn.

But she gave up medication for trance and meditation,
emptied her cupboards for the hungry on the streets.

She thought her cat a vegetarian and anyone could live
on water, grass, and air with proper breath control.

Perception so acute, she lived seven lives at once.
The only limits she'd accept—sunrise, sunset.

She took the bullet train, speeding toward the West.
Those left behind? Ah, well, they could take the bus.

Lollipop Man

Grape vines crept up the walls
and along the water pipes.
Mud turtles fertilized
their eggs beneath the stove.
In the hall in a bathtub
a piranha splashed a greeting
to One-Eyed,
One-Fingered,
One-Legged Larry,
favorite of the children—
Lollipop Man.

He came a day late,
climbed up the stairwell,
hand over hand,
rang the doorbell, hopped
to the table, filled up his plate,
burped with contentment.
Then he wiped off his mustache
with a pink party napkin.
When he found his other leg,
he said, "I never noticed."
Stole the clock and ran.

Advice to Writers: Sure-Fire Topics
for Best Sellers

How to crochet a coverlet using instructions
that include chaos theory;

How, when eating double lamb chops
in the back seat of a Mercedes,
to convince a Malamute to release
his jaws from around your wrist;

How to slide down the bannister
at the Waldorf
without ruining your panty hose
or firing your revolver;

How to reserve a table at the Palm Court
on the afternoon when only Pomeranians
are invited for tea;

How to engage a golden merman
with popsicles, or photographs,
as he swims up the path
through Prospect Park;

How to spend the summer joyously
in New Hampshire
with twenty-seven relatives,
including ghosts;

How to accept graciously a PhD
when the wrong name is called out:
"Abby Digsby McCutchen."

.

Eight Years Old

for Katherine Marie, my grandchild
after "Mistress Margaret Hussey"
John Skelton

Katie is as cheerful
as chili in salsa,
gentle as a magpie
or eagle from Tulsa.
In silence or chatter,
in music or clatter,
her thoughts matter.
Enthusiastic,
fantastic,
elastic,
she's amazing,
no hair-raising
      feat fazing
her.
      An earful,
rarely tearful,
Katie is as cheerful
as chili in salsa,
neat as a catbird's nest
up in a catalpa,
loves society
with propriety
like Hermione.
Among the newest,
and goofiest
actors and flutists,
well said well read
with books under bed,
she's often ahead.
And that's not all.
She plays basketball.

PART III

Black Wings

I dream of black wings
rushing a spit of sand,
wind rising, tide roaring—

An old wooden boat, one oar,
seesaws on the dark waves
pulling on the anchor,

a narrow chain attached
to a ten gallon can
tossed up on the shore.

My mother, silent in her tweed
dog-walking coat, stands
some feet away. Even so,

her presence comforts me. She died
a year younger than I am now,
wind rising, tide roaring in.

Life Guard

for John

Each time you saw me
draw back into that night of loss,
you'd sneak down cellar steps
to your hidden stash
of stand-out yard sale jewelry
as if selected
for this very purpose.

Pick a hand, you'd say and there
on your palm, big as a butter plate,
a gewgaw of such heroic ugliness
you'd resuscitate my laughter.

Presents

Laundry load of grief,
soaked, tumbled,
bleached with tears,
hung below high blue,
snaps, flaps, billows;

filters light,
creates refuge,
hiding place,
collects scents,
lilacs, grass.

Oh, JB,
how you still
take care of me.

From Afar

Scent of roses and lilies swirl before her
as she enters the hallway, bracelets tinkling.
Behind her niqab, onyx eyes flash;
below her billowing black silk abaya,
stilettoes click on the marble floor.

Her hand with its slender, tapered fingers,
almond-shaped nails polished clear silver,
rests on the muscular arm of her husband,
in Western clothes, a god in disguise.
So he is to her who's devoted her life

to his every need, earning entrance to heaven.
Her power's revealed in the careful way
he guides her through the door of the clinic,
her secret skin known only to him, but
soon, all too soon, to a fleet of doctors

Jefferson Hospital Cafeteria

A tiny lady wears a houndstooth hat.
It complements white hair, tan skin, brown eyes,

reflects her blouse's checks of picnic red
and white outlined by bright blue vines.

She scrapes her spoon around her yogurt cup,
then dips into her applesauce. All gone.

She sips her coffee, peering at the clock
above the elevator. Still time left

before she sees the ninth-floor specialist.
She takes a magnifying glass, unfolds

a well-worn schedule for the afternoon
train ride home. By then, that great man

on the ninth floor may well have found
an answer to her prayers.

Easter

for Diana Kate

Huge blue-gray, green, or turquoise eyes
depending on the weather and the light.
Hair red gold or Irish setter burgundy
depending on the season.

Strong back, long arms to hug you with,
big hands that could span two octaves,
lithe waist, no movement ungraceful,

she'd skate down our quiet road to school,
six feet tall on roller blades,
captured in a newspaper photo
entitled *Sign of Spring.*

Playing field hockey, she'd steal the ball
fly down the field, a young Valkyrie
riding the October wind.

At fourteen she went with her buddies
on a January ski trip to Quebec.
A bad fall, bruised hip, hospital,
an infection and scraping of the bone.

She turned fifteen on Valentine's Day.
The entire junior varsity hockey team,
defying the rules crept two by two
into her hospital room.

"Mom, it was great to see them.
They were trying to be nice,
but they don't understand how sick I am."

On Easter morning, I heard these words:
"Congratulations, we saved your daughter's life
last night. Septicemia. The fever finally broke."
I had not known until then that she could die.

The Djinn

for my ex-husband

Whose dark energy slams me awake?
Lightning flash, thunder crack.
Out of the night, a glimpse.
There, on the bridge, my ex-husband, fishing.

All he used to do was work, make things happen,
try to save the world, send wheat to Bangladesh.
I had never seen him cast a line before—
so patient.

On the bridge over the inlet
the fisherman still waits.
The hook at the end of the line
shimmers through dark waters.

Mindfulness

Be mindful every moment of your life,
the lady philosopher from Cambridge advises.

Slamming down the book, each word a knife,
she sees the gray scuff on the white stair risers,
the drooping curtain in need of a stitch,
the whole house embodying her complaint,
the greasy smudge on the hall light switch,
the long scrape where the stretcher tore the paint.

She'd rather not be *mindful*, thank you very much,
though each room oppresses with its musty smell.
She could set them right. She used to have the touch.
But how to rearrange all that had not gone well?

How could anyone? Perhaps dust particles were the sum,
a galaxy of neurons, of those years of sorrow.
Was she the only one to blame?
                      She hauls out the vacuum,
plugs it in for attack,
                    mindful of tomorrow.

Throwing Out Cookbooks

What former self recorded ways
for whipping up a cheese fondue
or roasting beef for holidays
to follow after oyster stew?

Who made from scratch this Hollandaise
for artichokes and cauliflower?
For chops and steaks this sauce Béarnaise
with vinegar for touch of sour?

Who collected in a tidy file
some seventy recipes for cake?
(Piles of frosting was her style
to hide the spots that didn't bake.)

Who would have been a super cook
had once she'd tried a new dish twice?
(Last Thanksgiving we partook
of tabbouleh, tofu, quinoa, rice.)

An Ordinary Button

Not a snap,
not a hook and eye,
not a zipper,
certainly not Velcro,
and not as cute
as that button
dropped from a
12th story window,
nor as bright as that one,
eaten by acid,
lost, blinking,
there, in the alley,
nor as shiny as the one
swallowed by mistake
with a handful of pills,
but an ordinary button,
hardened through
happenstance,
pokes through
the buttonhole,
earth and sky,
one generation to another.

Restoration

I went walking at low tide through high Spartina grass
and encountered eye to eye a thumb-sized frog who met me
with a stare. I never will forget his glaring outraged air,
so like my old professor in his green eye shade
when I betrayed my ignorance or made a thoughtless error.
Somehow this minute champion knew I meant no harm.
Sharing the power of his calm, he became my intercessor.
I thanked him and withdrew from his sharp-bladed tower.

Glimpse

You leaned down to kiss me,
your eyes not blue
but a chasm of color.
Earth's millennium shift
seen
within a canyon,
a dark ravine
open to sky.
Your long passage
through a wilderness of shadow
lit from below
by a river of laughter.

Afterwards

for JSB (1933-2012)

About all the pineapples in the world
or the sun on the leaves
or the leaves in the wind
or the wind on the waves
or the white caps springing
or the children running down
to the sea to meet them
I find you singing
in my mind.

About the Author

Adele earned her BA from Bryn Mawr College, attended the Harvard Graduate School of Education, moved to Washington, D.C., worked for a U.S. Representative, and then for GWETA's first educational television program, *Time for Science*. She married, had three children, moved to New York, divorced, worked for the World Law Fund and then taught English, theater, and directed the arts program at the same private school in Bedford, NY, she had attended as a child. She also completed her MA at Columbia Teachers College, then luckily remarried and moved with her new husband, John Setliffe Bourne, a computer whiz as well as a fellow poet, to Moorestown, NJ, where they lived for the next 38 years .

In New Jersey, Adele served as teacher/coordinator of a gifted and talented program, working with children from first grade through high school. She also taught English Composition at Burlington County College and Philadelphia College, her students including Marines at McGuire Air Base and sailors on nuclear subs at the Philadelphia Naval Base. Then, as time allowed, she served as president of Burlington County Poets and as literary editor of underAGE, a children's literary magazine published by the Princeton Arts Council. Courses with the poet Stephen Dunn at Stockton College spurred Adele and John to participate in the Philadelphia-Princeton literary scene, giving readings and publishing their poems, occasionally winning a prize or two.

In 2010, John edited a chapbook of Adele's work, *A Grocery List and Other Poems,* which was published by Finishing Line Press. But illness kept him from producing his own book. After his death in 2012, Adele moved to Providence, RI, to be near her daughter and her family. In 2014, she edited John's collection, *To Make A Thing of Air,* three books in one—"Poems for a Small Planet," a lifetime of poems, "The Professor Wanted Apples"—his humorous poems, and "A Mind of Winter", his last poems. Nancy Scott, who had suggested doing the book after John's memorial service—which had been filled with laughter and his poetry—was of invaluable help. The book was published by Steven R. Porter and designed by Dawn M. Porter of Stillwater River Publications. The Porters are the founders of the Association of Rhode Island Authors. Through membership in A.R.I.A. Adele has met fellow poets and through them other groups such as Frequency Writers and The Poets' Loft.

Many readers have reported that John's book, *To Make a Thing of Air*, had helped them through tough times. Just so, John's poetry led Adele to find a new life in a new city—and the desire to keep on writing. One result is this book: *Tide Roaring In.*

Made in the USA
Middletown, DE
29 October 2016